The shell house at Hampton Court House in Middlesex was designed by the astronomer, architect and garden-designer Thomas Wright in the 1750s for the Earl of Halifax, then the Ranger of nearby Bushey Park, and his mistress, the opera singer Mrs Donaldson.

Shell Houses and Grottoes

Hazelle Jackson

A Shire book

Published in 2001 by Shire Publications Ltd,
Cromwell House, Church Street, Princes Risborough,
Buckinghamshire HP27 9AA, UK.
(Website: www.shirebooks.co.uk)

British Library Cataloguing in Publication Data:
Jackson, Hazelle
Shell houses and grottoes. – (A Shire album; 398)
1. Shells 2. Cave architecture 3. Caves
I. Title
729.6
ISBN 0 7478 0522 9

Front cover: *The eighteenth-century limestone grotto at Painshill Landscape Garden, Surrey.*
Back cover: *A shell house for the Duke of Bedford built by Sir Jeffry Wyatville in 1811 in the grounds of Woburn Abbey, Bedfordshire.*

ACKNOWLEDGEMENTS

Photographs are acknowledged as follows: from the Buckinghamshire County Museums collections, page 16 (top); Charles Francis, page 28 (bottom); by courtesy of the Trustees of Goodwood House, page 11 (bottom); Gwyn Headley, page 18 (centre); National Trust, page 25 (top); Michael Symes, page 18 (bottom); by kind permission of the Marquess of Tavistock and the Trustees of the Bedford Estate, page 3. Mrs Peggy Stembridge kindly read the proofs and provided information about Goldney Grotto.

Printed in Malta by Gutenberg Press Limited, Gudja Road,
Tarxien PLA 19, Malta.

Contents

The indoor shell room at Woburn Abbey, Bedfordshire, is the oldest example of its type in Britain. It is believed to have been designed by Isaac de Caus in 1626 and was originally open on one side.

Early grottoes

And after having remained at the entry some time, two contrary emotions arose in me, fear and desire, fear of the threatening dark grotto, desire to see whether there were any marvellous things within it.

Leonardo da Vinci (1459–1513)

The seventeenth-century palazzo on Isola Bella ('Beautiful Island') in Lake Maggiore, Italy, has long been celebrated for its hanging gardens and grottoes. Below ground level, the grotto rooms provide a cool retreat from the summer sun. The walls are decorated with chips of black basalt, creamy 'spugne' and red marble, and the floors are set with pebbles.

The earliest grottoes were shrines, built in natural caves at the sites of sacred springs in ancient Greece, to honour the resident water spirits. Over time these shrines evolved into temples; in Greek a *nymphaeum* is a temple dedicated to water nymphs. Grottoes were popular in ancient Rome and the Romans used the term *nymphaeum* for both formal temples and artificial grottoes built around public fountains. Smaller domestic *nymphaea* were also built in Roman villas and gardens.

In ancient Rome the sea caves around the Bay of Naples, associated with the goddess Venus, were used for dining and entertaining and inspired a maritime style of grotto. Grottoes in honour of Venus were built with a half dome over an apse to symbolise the birth of Venus from a scallop shell. Inside, a statue of the goddess herself presided over tumbling water in a setting of mosaics, shells and sea coral. Roman grottoes were also

constructed at the site of natural calciferous springs, common in Italy, where the water bubbling out of the ground forms porous tufa deposits.

Architects in Renaissance Italy revived the grottoes of ancient Rome to add an air of historical authenticity to their neo-classical villas and gardens. The celebrated Renaissance architect Leon Battista Alberti even gives a 'recipe' in *De Re Aedifactoria* (1485) for pouring green molten wax on to the stonework of a new grotto to simulate mossy growth. Renaissance grottoes were decorated with chips of lava rock and coloured marble, shells, coral, pebbles and *spugne* – plaster textured to resemble coral. Many contained fanciful statues of beasts and gods inspired by the *Metamorphoses* of Ovid.

Renaissance gardens were designed with complex iconography. Francesco Colonna's mythic romance, *The Dream of Polyphilus* (1499), which describes the hero's search for self-knowledge in an enchanted classical landscape, was the theme for a number of allegorical gardens where a grotto with a water source was reached at the top of a terraced hillside, signifying the visitor's spiritual journey through life to knowledge.

Above: *The Grotta Grande was created in the Boboli gardens in Florence, Italy, in the sixteenth century by Bernardo Buontalenti. The simulated coral used is a form of plasterwork called 'spugne', a popular device on Italian grottoes.*

Right: *The gardens and grotto of the Villa Gamberaia at Settignano in Italy were originally laid out in the seventeenth century. A decorative wall niche contains a Rococo statue of a musician in a shell, tufa and 'spugne' setting.*

Renaissance engineers also exploited discoveries in hydraulics to add an element of surprise and theatre to gardens, creating *giochi d'aqua* (water jokes), automata and sound effects in elaborate artificial grottoes which combined elements of the *nymphaeum* and the sea cave.

The water courtyard of the sixteenth-century Villa Cicogna Mozzoni at Bisuschio in Italy has grotto niches with concealed jets of water that were turned on to drench unsuspecting visitors as they toured the gardens – a popular form of Italian practical joke.

5

By the seventeenth century the influence of the Renaissance had spread out across Europe and reached the British Isles. The first British grottoes were built as indoor rooms, often in the area beneath the stairs leading to the first-floor reception rooms, on the main floor, or the *piano nobile*, in a neo-classical villa. An early indoor grotto exists at Chatsworth House, Derbyshire, where in 1692 the first Duke of Devonshire converted the area beneath the grand stairs into a grotto-room with a fountain and a bas-relief of the goddess Diana bathing. There is a plain grotto-room under the entrance stairs behind Osterley House in west London.

Soon shells began to be used for decoration and two elaborate examples of early-seventeenth-century shell rooms have survived at Woburn Abbey in Bedfordshire (1626) and Skipton Castle in Yorkshire (1627). These are lined with ormer shells, mussels and mother-of-pearl in elaborate designs depicting sea dolphins, waves and mythical creatures, and are attributed to Isaac de Caus, a French Huguenot who, with his relative Salomon de Caus, was among the leading garden-designers and engineers of the early seventeenth century. He is recorded in the Works Accounts of 1623–4 as creating a shell grotto in the

Above: *The gatehouse at Skipton Castle in North Yorkshire, c.1627, contains one of only two surviving early-seventeenth-century shell rooms in Britain (the other is at Woburn Abbey in Bedfordshire). Both are believed to be the work of Isaac de Caus, a French Huguenot designer of gardens and grottoes.*

Right: *Isaac de Caus specialised in elaborate shellwork with mythical figures and a maritime theme. The Guernsey ormer shells and Jamaican coral used in Skipton Castle's shell room are said to have been collected by George Clifford, the third Earl of Cumberland, an Elizabethan admiral.*

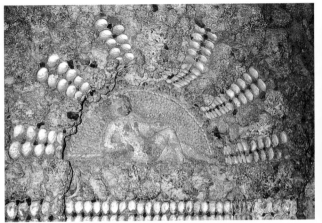

The terraces, tunnel and bath-house at Albury Park, Surrey, were designed by John Evelyn in the 1660s and originally the tunnel led out to the main London road. By 1819 the tunnel had fallen in, but it was later reopened by the new estate owner, Henry Drummond, the banker. There is no access today.

cellars of Inigo Jones's Banqueting Hall at Whitehall Palace to be a drinking den for King James I. His celebrated water theatre and grotto at Wilton House in Wiltshire were swept away by later generations. Salomon de Caus worked in England from about 1607–8 to 1613, initially for James I's queen, Anne of Denmark, and then from 1610 for her son Henry, Prince of Wales. In 1615 he published his influential masterpiece *Les Raisons des Eaux Mouvants*, demonstrating how to create complex water-powered automata and sound effects in fantastical grottoes using hydraulic principles derived from the engineers of antiquity like Hero of Alexandria (60–120).

In 1642, as Civil War broke out across England, the second Earl of Arundel, a leading Roman Catholic, left England with his family for Italy, where he was joined by the diarist John Evelyn (1620–1706). Evelyn travelled widely in Italy, studying architecture and garden-design, and on his return to England designed Italian-style gardens for his family and friends. In the 1660s Evelyn and Henry Howard, the Earl's grandson, remodelled Howard's grounds at Albury Park near Guildford as a Renaissance garden. Inspired by the grotto at Posilippo in Italy, reputed to be Virgil's tomb and admired by Evelyn on his travels, they drove a 160 yard (146 metre) tunnel into the hillside. In front of the tunnel they constructed an *exedra* (a semicircular structure with niches for statuary) and pool and, on the terraces below, a Roman bath-house or grotto. These have survived to the present day although the bath-house is now devoid of its original decoration.

Grottoes in the eighteenth century

In the eighteenth century wealthy Britons, finishing their education on the Grand Tour, identified close parallels between Ancient Rome and the burgeoning British Empire, and returned home with a passion for classical art and architecture and Arcadian landscapes. With seemingly limitless funds at their disposal, they set about recreating on their own estates some of the neo-classical splendours they had seen abroad, changing the style of British architecture and landscape for ever.

One of the most celebrated surviving examples of early-eighteenth-century garden-design is at Stowe in Buckinghamshire. In 1715 Viscount Cobham, newly returned from active service on the Continent, embarked upon the recreation of a classical landscape on his estate, taking as his theme an essay by the diarist Joseph Addison in *The Tatler* (number 123, 21st January 1710) about an allegorical dream in which virtue, honour and vanity are represented by buildings in a huge wood. He commissioned a number of classical-style temples (the family name was Temple) on the themes of liberty and tyranny, to reflect his views on the politics of the day. In the 1730s Lord Cobham hired William Kent, the landscape gardener and artist, to design a grotto at the head of the Serpentine river. Kent created a square cross-vaulted chamber with a statue of Venus in a central recess, the water flowing through a series of basins into the river in a style reminiscent of

Below left: Dating from the 1720s, the Rustic House is one of the oldest buildings in the gardens at Chiswick House in west London. The ornamental masonry simulates grotto construction of the period and inside are three niches for statues. The Rustic House was undergoing restoration when this photograph was taken.

Below: *The derelict brick façade of the grotto at Carshalton Park, Surrey, gives no hint of its former glory. Built in the 1720s over springs that fed the river Wandle, the grotto was decorated with flint, glass, lead, coral and shells to represent a sea cave. The central chamber had a marble seashell basin, and a statue of Neptune presided over the top of the arch. The nearby Carshalton House also has a grotto in the grounds.*

The grotto at Stowe, Buckinghamshire, was designed by William Kent in the 1730s. Originally neo-classical in style, it was covered with tufa and rockwork later in the eighteenth century to give it a more rustic and subterranean appearance, in keeping with the prevailing fashion for the picturesque.

Left: A view of Pope's villa, Twickenham, Middlesex, in 1807, shortly before it was demolished by its owner, Baroness Howe, to discourage sightseers, to the dismay of Pope's admirers. The entrance to the grotto can be seen in the centre of the ground floor below the stairs to the main reception rooms on the 'piano nobile'.

Below: The plan of the original layout of Pope's Grotto. It was made in 1785 by Pope's gardener, John Serle, as a guide for tourists.

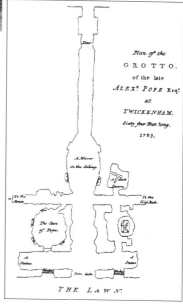

early Roman grottoes to Venus. Originally used as a banqueting house for light refreshments, the grotto at Stowe was remodelled later in the eighteenth century to give it the rustic and subterranean appearance by then fashionable for grottoes. Today Stowe is justly famous as being one of the world's first and finest landscape gardens.

The poet Alexander Pope (1688–1744), a leading influence on garden-design of the period, was a regular visitor to Stowe while it was being laid out. Pope never left England but between 1720 and 1725 he created a garden with classical allusions in the grounds of his riverside house on the Thames in Twickenham. In the tunnel under the road that links the house and the garden Pope built a grotto leading to a shell temple and decorated it with shells, glass and mirrors. Pope's grotto and garden were much visited and admired in the eighteenth century.

9

Left: *At Stourhead in Wiltshire the gardens were laid out to reflect a classical theme. In a cave adjoining the main chamber of the grotto a river god commands the river source and his nymphs and points out the way ahead.*

Above: *In the eighteenth century the fashionable estate-owner designed the views from selected vantage points on a tour of his grounds. At Stourhead the visitor looks out from the pagan setting of the grotto to the Christian church in the distance.*

The *nymphaeum*

The flint grotto at Clandon Park, Guildford, Surrey, is said to be the work of 'Capability' Brown in the 1770s. It houses a statue of the Three Graces and a water feature.

The Roman *nymphaeum* continued to provide the inspiration for many grottoes during the first half of the eighteenth century. One of the finest examples is the Grade I listed grotto at Stourhead in Wiltshire. Here in the 1740s the banker Henry Hoare dammed the river Stour to create a lake, and he commissioned Henry Flitcroft to construct a series of neo-classical buildings around it depicting scenes from *The Aeneid*. The grotto (*c.*1748) is a high-domed rocky chamber, lined with tufa; inside, a white lead statue by John

Cheere of the nymph Ariadne reclines on a marble plinth above a cold bath fed by the source of the river Stour. Inscribed on the basin's rim are verses, translated by Pope, dedicated to the 'Nymph of the Grot'.

At Clandon Park near Guildford, Surrey, a more modest *nymphaeum*, attributed to 'Capability' Brown in the 1770s, takes the form of a flint-and-brick cave with a statue of the Three Graces and a small pool.

The shell grotto and house

During the eighteenth century the formality of the early neo-classical gardens was quickly superseded by the movement to improve on nature, which resulted in the English landscape garden. Capability Brown and his disciples were called in to sweep away the old deer parks and formal gardens and replace them with rolling swathes of grassland, serpentine lakes and artfully placed clumps of trees. To enhance a view, create a mood and lend interest to a tour of the grounds, the fashionable landowner added a range of fantasy buildings or follies to his newly remodelled park. Eye-catchers, obelisks, temples, pagodas, ruins, towers, Chinese bridges and hermitages were scattered around the grounds and to complete the set a grotto, usually rustic in style, was added and lined with shells.

The grotto at Marble Hill Park, Twickenham, Middlesex, was built in the late 1730s by Henrietta Howard, Countess of Suffolk, with advice from her neighbour, the poet Alexander Pope. After being 'lost' for many years, its location was exposed when a tree fell on it in the great storms of 1987. It has since been partially restored by English Heritage.

Throughout the eighteenth century a veritable passion for shells raged among the rich and fashionable; rare shells were imported, bid for at auction, purchased at inflated prices from dealers and cajoled from fellow grotto-owners. Grottoes swallowed vast quantities of shells and many wealthy grotto-builders spent small fortunes importing exotic shells from around the world, particularly the West Indies. In 1739 Captain Knowles of HMS *Diamond* brought in a shipload of shells for the Dukes of Richmond and Bedford and in 1788 Lord Donegal had £10,000 worth of shells waiting to be unpacked. The larger and more exotic a grotto's shells, the more they excited envy and admiration. Even the earliest grottoes had lists of specimens. Owners visited each other's grottoes to admire or criticise the design and workmanship and to study and covet unusual specimens. It seems that everybody in the eighteenth century had an opinion on grottoes: 'Mine is prettier than Mr Pope's,' said Lady Hertford in 1736 of her grotto at Marlborough, Wiltshire.

The Grade I listed shell house at Goodwood House, Sussex, was created in the 1740s by the Duchess of Richmond and her daughters, with local shells and exotic imports from Jamaica. It was restored between 1989 and 1995 by Diana Reynell and Roger Capps, using over 55,000 shells from Britain and Cuba.

The Grade I listed grotto at Goldney Hall, Bristol, is one of the finest eighteenth-century shell grottoes in Britain. It was built by Thomas Goldney, a local merchant, between 1737 and 1764 and contains thousands of exotic shells, many from the West Indies. See page 34 for a detail of this grotto.

The shells for the Duke of Richmond were used in the 1740s to construct a shell house at Goodwood, his country estate in Sussex. This is a rustic pavilion sited high on a windy ridge with views across the Downs towards the distant sea. Inside, a rectangular room is encrusted with shells arranged with breathtaking geometric precision. Mirrors bounce the sunlight off the walls, which appear to ripple in the reflected light. The Duchess of Richmond and her daughters, Lady Caroline and Lady Emily, are said to have spent seven years on its construction and Lady Emily later created another shell room at Carton in County Kildare in Ireland following her marriage to the Duke of Leinster in 1747.

A complex shell house or grotto could take decades for an obsessive owner to create. The shell grotto at Goldney Hall, Bristol, one of the finest surviving eighteenth-century grottoes, was built between 1737 and 1764 by Thomas Goldney, a wealthy merchant. Here, in a vaulted subterranean chamber encrusted with exotic shells and lustrous minerals, a statue of a

Above: *Scott's Grotto at Ware in Hertfordshire has many chambers lined with shells, all dug out of the chalk hillside in the mid eighteenth century. The grotto was saved from the developer's bulldozers at the last minute in the 1980s (the porch had already been demolished when the preservation order was served). It has since been restored by the local council and the Ware Society.*

Right: *This map of Scott's Grotto was prepared by Mr R. T. Andrews of East Hertfordshire Archaeological Society in 1900 to guide visitors through the maze of subterranean passages in the chalk.*

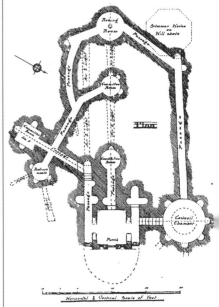

A plan of the grotto made in 1900 by Mr R.T. Andrews, of the East H Archaeological Society – with amendments to show the new porch.

The shell grotto at Margate, Kent, contains a central chamber reminiscent of early pagan shrines, which has contributed to the belief that the grotto is a Mithraic temple dating from the Roman occupation of Britain.

maritime god presides over a tumbling cascade, originally powered by a steam-driven pump in a nearby tower.

At Ware in Hertfordshire in the 1750s and 1760s the Quaker poet John Scott excavated a series of chambers reaching nearly 70 feet (20 metres) into his chalk hillside garden and lined them with shells. His puritanical brother disapproved, but London society flocked to see it and Dr Johnson pronounced it 'a fairy hall'.

A shell grotto was discovered accidentally at Margate, Kent, in 1835 by the son of a local schoolmaster, Mr Newlove, who was excavating the hillside above it. No records of its construction have ever been found. Some historians maintain it is a 'secret' grotto, built by Lady Holland in the eighteenth century, while others claim it is a Mithraic temple built by soldiers stationed on the Isle of Thanet in the days of the Roman Empire.

Where the ground was unsuitable for excavation, shell houses made an attractive alternative. A shell house might be a purpose-built,

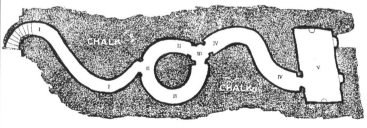

THE PLAN OF THE GROTTO

The orientation is almost exactly north and south, reading laterally from the entrance passage to the end chamber.

I. Entrance.   II. Rotunda.   III. The Dome.   IV. Serpentine Passage.   V. Altar Chamber.

This distance from the top of the steps to the end wall of the shrine is 104ft. the rough entrance passage made by Mr. Newlove being 36ft. in length and the Grotto proper 68ft.

The shell-lined passage at Margate extends 68 feet (20 metres) into the chalk and its serpentine design adds to its mystery.

13

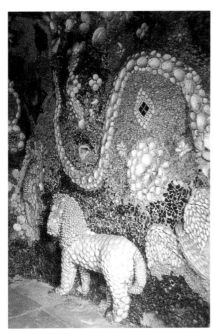

Above: *The origins and date of the shell house at Tapeley Park in Devon are unknown but it is believed to be eighteenth-century. There are rustic branches around the doors and a pebble floor.*

Left: *The charming shellwork at Walhampton House (now Hordle Walhampton School), Hampshire, was applied in the 1780s by the former coxswain of the estate-owner, Admiral Sir Harry Burrard-Neale.*

rustic-style pavilion, or a conversion of an existing garden building. In the 1780s Admiral Sir Harry Burrard-Neale employed his former coxswain to create a shell house in the grounds of Walhampton House, Boldre, Hampshire. It is said that on completion of the work, with nothing more to live for, the coxswain drowned himself in the Solent. There are eighteenth-century shell houses at Hatfield Forest, Essex, and Tapeley Park, Devon. At Mount Edgcumbe in Cornwall a rare eighteenth-century shell-decorated garden seat survives.

The Rococo movement, at its height on the Continent in the mid eighteenth century, drew its inspiration from shells, with their

The rare eighteenth-century shell seat in the Earl's Garden at Mount Edgcumbe in Cornwall was restored in the 1980s by Diana Reynell, who used crystalline rocks from Devon to rebuild the finial on the top.

Above: The rustic shell house in the Rococo garden at Hampton Court House, Middlesex, is built from furnace slag and unusual mineral specimens. A nearby icehouse is built in the same style and there are remains of similar rustic buildings by the heart-shaped lake and in the ruined winter garden.

Right: Many of the shells at Hampton Court House originated from the West Indies. It was restored with English Heritage funding by Diana Reynell after it was damaged by a falling tree in the storms of 1987.

swirling stylised patterns applied to furniture, architecture and decoration. A leading exponent of the style in England was Thomas Wright of Durham (1711–86), an astronomer who turned to architecture and garden-design, and whose wealthy patrons included the Earl of Halifax. One of Wright's most notable Rococo designs is Hampton Court House in Middlesex, built in 1757 for the Earl's mistress, the beautiful opera singer Anna Maria Donaldson. In the grounds Wright built a shell house overlooking a heart-shaped lake. Many of the shells are from the West Indies, said to have been sent back by Mrs Donaldson's husband, who was a sea captain.

Shellwork was a popular and socially approved hobby for refined ladies throughout the eighteenth century. One of its most celebrated female exponents was Mrs Mary Delany (1700–88). Before her second marriage she moved in court circles and was in demand as a companion in fashionable society for her charm and skill at embroidery and handicrafts. In 1731 she accompanied her close friend Mrs Donnellan on an extended visit to Mrs Donnellan's relatives at Killala in Ireland, where the party amused themselves by constructing a shell grotto. In 1736 she advised her uncle, Sir John Stanley, on his grotto at North End in London. Around this time she met her lifelong friend, the Duchess of Portland, who shared her interest in natural history and was herself a great collector of shells. In 1743 she married the Dean of Delville, Dr Patrick Delany, a friend of Swift and Pope, and moved to Ireland, where, encouraged by her husband, she continued to paint, embroider, create intricate shellwork and design her gardens at

Above: *During the late eighteenth century the noted grotto-builder Mrs Delany was a regular visitor to Bulstrode Park in Buckinghamshire, the country estate of her great friend the Duchess of Portland. In the 1770s the Duchess, a keen amateur naturalist, collected thousands of snail shells to decorate a grotto that she and Mrs Delany had built in the grounds. It was demolished in the nineteenth century.*

Delville and Downpatrick. She decorated the ceiling of the chapel at Delville with shellwork, creating flowers and swags with the shells set on edge so that the petals achieved the effect of stucco in high relief. The chapel was demolished in the 1940s.

Mrs Delany's advice on shellwork was sought by many friends. She is believed to have advised Sir Charles Mordaunt's daughters when they constructed the exquisite shell swags in the tea parlour above the bath-house grotto at Walton in Warwickshire in the 1750s. After she was widowed in 1768 Mrs Delany moved back to England and spent a good deal of time with the dowager Duchess of Portland at Bulstrode, the Duchess's country estate in Buckinghamshire, where they built a grotto in the 1770s (demolished in the late nineteenth century).

The use of shells to simulate internal plasterwork can also be seen at Basildon Park, Berkshire, and at A La Ronde outside Exmouth in Devon, where in the 1790s the Parminter ladies on their return from Europe designed a unique circular house with shell galleries.

The simulated limestone cave

In the late 1730s, after a visit to the West Country, Alexander Pope remodelled his grotto to give it a more natural, less stylised appearance, badgering friends and acquaintances for unusual stones and minerals. In 1742 Sir Hans Sloane sent him rock samples from the Giant's Causeway in Ireland; other specimens came from the Reverend Dr William Borlase of Camborne School

Far left: *The grotto at Painshill Park in Surrey was designed by the estate's owner, Charles Hamilton, in the 1750s. It is believed to be the first eighteenth-century grotto to simulate a natural limestone cave both internally and externally. Restoration began in the 1980s after a long period of dereliction.*

Left: *This statue of St James of Compostela, with a scallop shell in his hat, was found in Pope's Grotto at Twickenham, Middlesex, when the site was taken over by a school in the 1990s. It is believed to be of Italian origin and contemporary with the grotto itself.*

A walkway by the lake at Painshill, Surrey, leads down to the entrance to the grotto-complex on Grotto Island. The misshapen rocks are pinned to the underlying brick structure with iron pins.

of Mines in Cornwall. Pope continued to work on his grotto up to his death in 1744.

In the 1750s Charles Hamilton, a younger son of Lord Abercorn, created one of the century's finest Romantic gardens at Painshill in Surrey. At its heart he placed a glittering rock-and-crystal grotto, one of the first designed to simulate a natural limestone cave, both internally and externally, and which had a great impact on the style of grottoes in the second half of the eighteenth century. The influences behind Hamilton's grotto are undocumented but he is known to have visited the sea caves around Naples on the Grand Tour.

Painshill grotto is set on an island in the lake in the middle of the park. The central chamber is approached via a dark, winding tunnel, 20 yards (18 metres) long, the walls of which are covered with bands of gypsum flakes and purple fluorite crystals. Mock stalactites hang from the ceiling. Shells crunch underfoot. The only light is a dim green watery reflection from the lake through small slits in the rock. At the end of the passage there is a large rocky chamber overlooking the lake, decorated with more crystals and a stalactite-encrusted ceiling. As the visitor entered, the gardener, concealed in a side chamber, would turn an Archimedean screw, causing a small waterfall to crash down, the water trickling away into the rock pools on the floor.

The whole venture proved so expensive that Hamilton was forced to sell up and move to the West Country, where he continued to advise wealthy friends on garden-design and grotto-building, including the grotto-cascade at Bowood House in Wiltshire. The Painshill grotto survived into the twentieth century but was vandalised by troops during the Second World War. Later, the roof collapsed after the lead was stolen. In the 1990s restoration was begun in earnest by Diana Reynell.

Inside the grotto at Painshill, gypsum and feldspar chips and other crystalline minerals are overlapped on the walls to create the effect of limestone and are also stuck to formers to create artificial stalactites.

Right: *The cascade at Bowood House, Wiltshire, was designed for the Earl of Lansdowne by Charles Hamilton in the late eighteenth century. It was built by Joseph and Josiah Lane from Tisbury in Wiltshire, the leading English grotto-builders of the second half of the eighteenth century. The Lanes were also employed by Charles Hamilton to construct his grotto at Painshill.*

Below: *The Grade I listed grotto at Ascot Place, Berkshire, was built for Daniel Agace in the mid eighteenth century in a similar naturalistic style to its contemporaries at nearby Painshill and Oatlands Park. It is one of the best preserved grottoes anywhere. There is no public access.*

Another fine eighteenth-century grotto in a similar style to Painshill is at nearby Ascot Place in Berkshire, built for Daniel Agace in the 1740s. It has survived virtually intact to the present day. Little is known of its original architect or designer. Overlooking the lake near the house, the grotto has a number of rock-and-tufa chambers decorated with felspar stalactites, and zigzagged bands of minerals around the walls. (The Ascot Place grotto is private, with no public access.)

Not far away, at Oatlands in Surrey, a celebrated grotto was built in the 1760s and 1770s for the ninth Earl of Lincoln at a cost of over £40,000. This was a two-storey building with three rooms on the ground floor and an upstairs sitting-room accessible from the outside by a ramp and, like the Ascot Place grotto, with views over a lake. All the rooms were encrusted with spars, shells and stalactites. The house later became a hotel, and the grotto survived intact until 1948, when it was dynamited by the owners and the former Ministry of Works, who declared it a hazard to trespassers, despite a concerted campaign by supporters to save it.

The grottoes at Painshill, Ascot Place and Oatlands are all believed to be the work of Joseph and Josiah Lane of Tisbury, Wiltshire,

The two-storey grotto at Oatlands, Surrey, (c.1747) overlooked the lake. Zigzag bands of quartz and felspar were stuck to the walls and on to artificial stalactites to create the illusion of a natural limestone cave.

Left: *Joseph and Josiah Lane created the rock grotto at Old Wardour Castle in Wiltshire in the late eighteenth century. They may have removed some of the rocks from a local Neolithic circle to serve as building material.*

Right: *The Cleft is a narrow crevice leading up to the top of Grotto Hill at Hawkstone Park in Shropshire. It is believed to be a natural feature which Sir Rowland Hill had cleared of vegetation, having steps carved into it, when laying out the grounds as a sublime landscape park in the late eighteenth century.*

who worked in a naturalistic style and were among the most celebrated English grotto-builders of the eighteenth century. Towards the end of the eighteenth century the Lanes built the grotto-cascade (designed by Charles Hamilton) at Bowood House, Wiltshire, for the Marquis of Lansdowne and created the large rockwork grotto at Old Wardour Castle, Wiltshire, for a branch of the Arundell family.

At the end of the eighteenth century the Romantic Movement led to an interest in wild mountain scenery, and wealthy landowners remodelled their parks to reflect this. At Hawkstone Park in Shropshire between 1780 and 1825 the Hill family carved tunnels and grottoes out of the red sandstone hills to create a landscape designed to inspire fear and wonder in equal measure. To reach the summit of Grotto Hill, the visitor must clamber up a steep flight of steps carved into the base of a narrow-sided ravine and grope along a long dark tunnel to emerge at the top in a labyrinth of dim rock-carved chambers. These lead out to a precipitous cliff face called the Raven's Ledge. Originally the main chamber had stained-glass windows and was decorated with blue furnace slag, shells, pumice and tufa by the Misses Hill. After a long period of decline, the park was restored at the end of the twentieth century and is now once more open to the public.

Inside the labyrinth of rock chambers at the top of Grotto Hill at Hawkstone Park, the main chamber leads to the Raven's Ledge, a precipitous drop. The shells that once covered the walls have long since been removed.

19

Some fine mineral specimens can be observed in the Victorian grotto-arbour in the grounds of the late-eighteenth-century house at Belmont Park, Throwley, Kent, which was designed by Samuel Wyatt.

Grottoes in the nineteenth and twentieth centuries

A few shell houses were built in the early nineteenth century, notably those for the Duke of Bedford by Sir Jeffry Wyatville at Endsleigh in Devon (1810) and at Woburn in Bedfordshire (1811), but, increasingly, garden-owners built imitation caves in rockeries and incorporated unusual fossils and minerals into the

Far left and left: *Endsleigh shell house in Devon (1810) overlooks the Tamar valley. It was designed by Sir Jeffry Wyatville to complement the Repton house and grounds, a holiday home and fishing lodge belonging to the Duke of Bedford.*

Above: *Ammonites were popular in grottoes. These are on the floor of the grotto at Belcombe Court in Wiltshire.*

Right: *The grotto-cave at Pencarrow House, Bodmin, Cornwall, is concealed within an extensive nineteenth-century rockery. Its wall and roof contain minerals and fossil specimens.*

external walls. The Woburn shell house combines both fashions, with a shell interior and some fine mineral specimens in the external walls. At Belmont Park in Kent the nineteenth-century grotto-arbour is constructed from a variety of large and interesting mineral samples. Ammonites are set in the roof of the Hermit's Cave at Bowood and in the floor of the grotto at Belcombe Court in Wiltshire, and the grotto in the rockery at Pencarrow in Cornwall is a large cave with rocks and mineral specimens, including a large brain coral, embedded in the internal walls and ceiling.

One of the last nineteenth-century grottoes to be built in the old grotesque style of the eighteenth century can be found in Bath at the Bath Spa Hotel, previously Vellore House. The grotto was built in 1836 for General Augustus Andrews, lately retired from the Indian army. Constructed of perforated uncut Bath stone from nearby Combe Down, it was renovated at considerable expense in 1985 to be the focal point of the sweeping entrance-drive to the hotel.

This grotto-alcove at Stancombe Park, Gloucestershire, is in one of the many tunnels surrounding the lake. The Gothick garden at Stancombe is believed to date from the middle of the nineteenth century. The shells are contemporary – from Wheeler's restaurant in London.

Far left: *Sir George Staunton, an orientalist and MP for Portsmouth, created the gardens at Leigh Park, Hampshire, between 1820 and 1860. The shell house was originally encrusted with shells and pebbles in a design based on the Chichester cross, and a stonework crown once topped the roof. The park is now called Staunton Country Park.*

Left: *The entrance to the lakeside cave grotto at Belcombe Court in Wiltshire shows the concealed turn needed to enter the main chamber, where small frogs greet the unwary visitor.*

Technological inventions came thick and fast during the nineteenth century. The Wardian case, a portable greenhouse, allowed tender and exotic plants to be safely imported from overseas. In addition, the abolition of the Glass Tax in 1845, the repeal of the Window Tax in 1851, the availability of mass-produced glass and iron and improved hot-water systems enabled owners to build large greenhouses, which meant tender plants could be kept over the winter. Massed bedding schemes and exotic fern-filled conservatories became popular and in many Victorian gardens the only surviving legacy of the Georgian grotto was a rock tunnel linking two different areas of the garden to invoke a change of mood. Many of these 'grotto-tunnels' have a sharp curve

Far left and left: *The entrance to the Grade I listed rock grotto at Glansevern Hall, Powys, is via a low, unlit opening at one side of the back of the entrance arch. A sharp right turn is needed to enter the grotto, which twists along a rock passage to emerge at the other end of the semicircular rockery. The grotto dates from the 1840s and there are no shells inside, in keeping with the Victorian preference for more natural-looking rockwork.*

22

Left: *The tunnel at Biddulph Grange, Staffordshire, is at the end of the Scottish-glen garden. The visitor ventures into the dark, rocky tunnel past the (closed) entrance to the icehouse and emerges on the verandah of the red-and-gold Chinese temple overlooking the pond in the Chinese garden.*

Below right: *The Swiss Garden, Old Warden, Bedfordshire, is said to have been built by Lord Ongley in the 1830s for his Swiss mistress. The original grotto was remodelled to be a fernery and conservatory in the 1870s by Joseph Shuttleworth. The tufa walls and glass-domed roof were restored in the 1980s by Bedfordshire County Council.*

Right: *At Gyllyngdune Gardens, Falmouth, Cornwall, a small wooded chine in the cliffs has been turned into a dark glen with evergreens, Pulhamite rockwork and shell-lined seats. Once, it led down to the beach through shell caves under the road. The caves are now locked to the public.*

at the entrance, forcing the visitor to take a symbolic step into the darkness before being able to see the light at the other end. Examples exist at Ashridge in Hertfordshire, Endsleigh in Devon, Glansevern Hall in Powys and Biddulph Grange in Staffordshire.

Some earlier grottoes were adapted to reflect Victorian taste. In the 1870s James Shuttleworth converted Lord Ongley's 1830s grotto at the Swiss Garden, Old Warden, Bedfordshire, into a fernery, with a glass-roofed dome, stained-glass doors, and tufa-lined walls containing niches for the ferns. The restored Victorian fernery at Ascog on the Isle of Bute in Scotland has a sunken grotto-style entrance. By the end of the nineteenth century the flower-garden with its rockeries and massed bedding schemes and the fern-filled conservatory had usurped the eighteenth-century

23

Sheerness Grotto, Kent, owes its existence to the wreck of a ship carrying barrels of cement powder in the 1830s. The cement set and the salvaged barrels were rescued by a local farmer and used to form the main structure of the grotto, originally topped by ships' figureheads. The grotto can still be seen in the car park of the Ship on Shore public house.

Right: *Highnam Court in Gloucestershire has one of the largest early Pulhamite rock gardens in England with rockeries, water features and two grottoes. The underlying brick base used to construct Pulhamite rock can be clearly seen in the photograph.*

Left: *The Pulhamite cave at Sunningdale Park, Berkshire, is part of a large complex constructed by Major and Mrs Joicy in the early twentieth century. The house and grounds later became the Civil Service College.*

landscape garden, with its grassy lawns, indigenous plants, and whimsical follies and grottoes.

New building materials continued to be developed throughout the nineteenth century. In the late 1840s James Pulham devised a very realistic form of artificial boulder called Pulhamite, using a process in which cement is poured over masses of clinker and moulded into boulder-like artificial rock formations. Pulhamite rockwork was widely used right up to the early years of the twentieth century to build artificial caves and rockeries and can still be found in many gardens and parks including Waddesdon Manor in Buckinghamshire, Battersea Park in London, Merrow Grange in Guildford, and Highnam Court in Gloucestershire.

Rocaille work and tufa provide the setting for the statuary in the grotto-alcove that forms the centrepiece of the nineteenth-century aviary at Waddesdon Manor, Buckinghamshire.

Far left: The water gardens at Waddesdon Manor contain some fine Pulhamite rockwork. Here a path leads to a partly concealed cave entrance in the rocks.

Left: An Italian mosaic grotto-floor at Oakworth Park, West Yorkshire. The elaborate winter gardens, now a public park, were constructed by Sir Isaac Holden between 1869 and 1874 at a cost of £80,000.

Below: Fake stalactites were a popular element inside grottoes. These carved stalactites at Oakworth Park have lost their tips.

Below: *The Pulhamite 'Owl Cave' at Highnam Court, Gloucestershire, takes its name from a stone owl which sat on a niche in the back of the cave, until it was stolen. Another Pulhamite grotto overlooks the stream running through the grounds.*

THE LITTLE CHAPEL
AND ITS BUILDER,
LES VAUXBELETS, GUERNSEY.

Above left: *The Italianate gardens at Hever Castle, Kent, were built by Viscount Astor in the early twentieth century. The grotto-alcoves lining the Pergola Walk were inspired by the Gallery of a Hundred Fountains at the Renaissance Villa d'Este at Tivoli near Rome.*

Above right: *La Grotte at Les Vauxbelets in Guernsey is part grotto, part chapel. It was built in 1914, then enlarged in 1916 and 1923. The chapel, which is built over a simulation of the grotto at Lourdes, is composed of shells, fragments of china and other salvaged materials.*

Left: *Grosvenor Gardens, London, opposite Victoria station, contains two little shell-decorated gardeners' huts. They were built by the French government after the Second World War to aid the upkeep of the garden, which is dedicated to Marshal Foch.*

After the First World War the armies of labourers and gardeners who had worked for wealthy landowners were no longer available, and owners struggled to maintain their estates during the economic depression of the 1930s. The social changes wrought by the Second World War were greater still. Many historic houses were requisitioned by the armed forces and their grottoes, like that at Painshill, were vandalised by bored troops. In the post-war years, with punitive death duties imposed on inherited wealth, many once great estates were broken up and sold for housing. Shell houses and grottoes were ignored, neglected or bulldozed into oblivion.

The grotto designed by Quinlan Terry at West Green in Hampshire was home in the late 1990s to a large grass snake.

In the 1980s widespread car ownership helped membership of the National Trust soar to more than one million, and the government-owned historic property estate was reconstituted as English Heritage. An active retired population fostered growing public interest in garden history and a revival of interest in grottoes.

Between 1974 and 1980 the neo-classicist architect Quinlan Terry built a folly garden with a grotto and *nymphaeum* for Lord McAlpine at West Green in Hampshire. In 1986 one of the greatest grottoes since the eighteenth century was created by Vernon Gibberd, Diana Reynell and Simon Verity at Leeds Castle in Kent. Set beneath the maze, which has to be navigated to reach its entrance, the grotto unites all the elements of a Renaissance grotto: a cascade, a tunnel and elaborate shellwork featuring black swans, which are the symbol of Leeds Castle and represent alchemy.

Right and centre: *The subterranean grotto at Leeds Castle in Kent was designed by Vernon Gibberd in the 1980s. It is entered from the centre of a maze and leads down a twisting passage decorated with shells and occult imagery. The shellwork antelope and swans are by Diana Reynell. Swans are the symbol of Leeds Castle and are also associated with alchemy.*

The grotto overlooking the pond at Kingstone Cottages near Ross-on-Wye, Herefordshire, was built by the owner, Michael Hughes, in the 1980s. Entered via a twisting passage, the main chamber has a window that opens directly on to the pond.

Amateur grotto-builders also revived the form: in the late 1980s Michael Hughes created a shell grotto overlooking a pond at Kingstone Cottages outside Ross-on-Wye, Herefordshire. At Horton in Northamptonshire the late Gervase Jackson Stops restored the Menagerie, an eighteenth-century banqueting house by Thomas Wright, and created a shell room in the basement, reached by stepping-stones over black waters symbolising the river Styx.

In the late twentieth century Diana Reynell, an art teacher, restored the shell grotto at Marlborough and embarked on a career as a grotto-builder and restorer, reviving the tradition of the female grotto-builders of the

Far left and left: The eighteenth-century Menagerie at Horton in Northamptonshire was restored in the late twentieth century by Gervase Jackson Stops. In the cellars is a twentieth-century shell grotto entered over a dark pool (representing the river Styx) and guarded by Charon, the mythological boatman. Inside, fashioned with shells, lurk Cerberus, guardian of the underworld, and Apollo with his lyre.

The islands in the rockery at the Lost Gardens of Heligan in Cornwall have been reconstructed using unusual specimen rocks from different areas of Cornwall. On summer evenings candles were lit in the grotto, causing the crystals in the rocks to glitter and cast a soft glow over the rockery islands.

Far left: *The grotto at Portmeirion in north Wales is below the Belvedere. Facing the sea, it has a maritime feel, with oyster shells, a mermaid fountain and glass bottle tops reflecting the sunlight.*

Left: *A faun with pan-pipes in the shell grotto made by Peter and Wendy Dare in the 1980s at Mill Dene in Blockley, Gloucestershire. Water is piped over the top to create a cascade.*

eighteenth century. Other contemporary female grotto-builders include Belinda Eade, who worked with Diana Reynell on the restoration of the shell house at Hampton Court House and created the grotto at Nantclwyd Hall in Denbighshire, Wales, and Blot Kerr Wilson, a shell artist, who created exquisite shell houses at Ballymaloe House in Ireland and Belcombe Court in Wiltshire in the 1990s.

Nineteenth-century rock grottoes were also swept up in the revival of the form: major restorations included the grottoes at Heligan and Trevarno in Cornwall, at Glansevern in Powys, Wales, and at Carr Bank Park, Mansfield, Nottinghamshire.

Grottoes can be built anywhere – cellars, bathrooms, conservatories or back gardens. They can be as small as a rockwork fountain in a conservatory or as large as an excavated purpose-built cave lined with shells. Once again, in the twenty-first century as in the eighteenth, the only limits are the budget and the imagination of the owner.

Intricate shellwork was added to the original eighteenth-century pavilion at Belcombe Court in Wiltshire by the shell artist Blot Kerr Wilson in the 1990s. Belcombe also has a 'grotesque' rock grotto with a central cave overlooking the lake.

Design, construction and decoration

Design

Pattern books for follies including grottoes were published throughout the eighteenth century and William Wrighte's *Grotesque Architecture or Rural Amusement* (1767) includes plans,

elevations and sections for 'Chinese, Gothic and Natural Grottoes, Mosques, Moresque Pavilions, and Summer and Winter Hermitages'. Aspiring grotto-owners could visit other grottoes to consult and discuss designs and hire designers like William Kent and Thomas Wright. A number of Thomas Wright's well-connected patrons, including the Duke of Beaufort, the Earl of Halifax and Mrs Delany, subscribed to the two-part publication of his designs for arbours and grottoes in *Universal Architecture* (1755 and 1758).

Rustic- and grotesque-style exteriors were popular, with the use of flints, irregular stones, crooked branches and bark-covered surfaces. In the late eighteenth and early nineteenth centuries the rustic style was often combined with Gothick Revival features, like pointed window- and door-frames, and stained-glass windows. The apogee of this style can be seen in the shell-lined Gothick hermitage on the hilltop in Pontypool Park, Wales.

Above left: Goldney Grotto, Bristol, is subterranean. A flight of steps leads down to an early-Gothic entrance. It can be reached via a yew avenue from the house or via a second entrance with a winding tunnel under the great terrace to the main chamber.

Left: The grotto-hermitage at Pontypool Park in south Wales has rustic timberwork, shell-decorated walls and ceiling, Gothick windows and a fireplace. A hermit is said to have taken up residence there for a time during the nineteenth century.

Below: The grotto-hermitage at Pontypool Park is one of the best shell houses in Wales. Set on a windy ridge, it is believed to have been converted from an earlier hunting lodge by the Hanbury family in the early nineteenth century.

Above: *Dido's Temple at Stowe, Buckinghamshire. Like the grotto at Stowe, the original early-eighteenth-century classical-style building was altered in the late eighteenth century, by pinning tufa and misshapen rocks to the exterior, to make it look more picturesque.*

Right: *The flint-lined grotto-tunnel at Ashridge, Hertfordshire, leads to different themed areas of the Repton gardens. Originally a cascade tumbled over the rocks on the path leading to the entrance.*

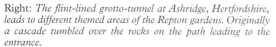

Construction

Natural materials, like bark and tree trunks, and local building materials were used in the construction of a grotto: the grotto-hermitage at Carshalton House, Surrey, (1720s) is made of the local white chalk clunch, while the *nymphaeum* at Clandon Park, also in Surrey, (1770s) is built with local flints and red brick. There are tree trunks prominent in the entrances at Pontypool Park and at Tapeley Park in Devon.

Often the underlying structure of the grotto was built with local bricks and dressed with 'grotesque' rocks or 'holey' limestone, pinned on with iron pins and stuck in place with lime mortar. At Painshill the distinctive limestone used to dress the brickwork came from the west of England. Goldney Grotto in Bristol is made from burnt bricks dressed with spongestone and tufa. At Ashridge in Hertfordshire the grotto, built of local pudding-stone, has a tunnel that is lined with local flints pinned to the roof and walls.

Recycled furnace slag was popular with grotto-builders for its resemblance to Italian volcanic lava. Examples can be seen at Marlborough, Goldney and Warmley grottoes and at Hampton Court House shell house. Much of the slag has a blue glassy appearance caused by the use of copper in eighteenth-century furnaces. The more expensive grottoes incorporated unusual mineral specimens in their external walls, and a fine selection can be seen in the shell house at Woburn Abbey, Bedfordshire (*c.*1811). The unusual limestone used at Painshill can also be seen on the shell house at Hampton Court House and the ruined grotto at Wanstead Park in east London.

Far left: *Detail of the rockwork at Painshill, Surrey, showing the distinctive 'holey' limestone used to dress the basic brick structure. The holes in the rock are a natural feature believed to have been bored by marine molluscs called piddocks.*

Left: *Furnace slag was widely used as a grotto-building material and was popular for its cheapness and its resemblance to Italian volcanic lava. Here it is used on an entrance and tunnel at Goldney Grotto in Bristol.*

Decoration

Many grottoes took years to build, changing to reflect different styles of garden design during the eighteenth century. Many owners copied elements of Italian grottoes, which were decorated with inlaid coloured marble (white and green were popular), unusual minerals, coral, glossy black lava stone, pebbles and tufa. Marble and lava chips were not widely available in Britain and

Left: *Unusual rocks and mineral samples were used to construct the exterior of the shell house at Woburn, Bedfordshire, in 1811*

Below: *The 'holey' limestone or 'pierre antediluvienne' used at Painshill, Surrey, was much sought after for grottoes and can also be found around the doorways at Hampton Court House shell house, Middlesex. Examples have also been found in the ruined grotto at Wanstead Park, east London, and in a number of other rustic eighteenth-century buildings.*

Left: *A maritime god sits at the head of a tumbling cascade in Goldney Grotto, Bristol. Towards the end of construction a steam-driven pump was installed in a nearby tower, possibly replacing an earlier windmill, to raise the water for the cascade.*

Below: *A shell-lined seat at Scott's Grotto, Ware, Hertfordshire, in the main room, known as the Council Chamber.*

Above left: *Artificial stalactites often hung from grotto ceilings. These were often made from timber formers coated with lime plaster, with shells and other materials pressed into it while the plaster was still wet. This process can be seen in the restoration of Charles Hamilton's grotto at Painshill, Surrey.*

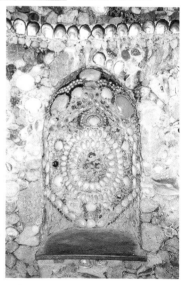

grotto-builders had to improvise and substitute local materials. At Painshill, hothouse cinders are stuck to the lower walls of the entrance tunnel and main chamber to simulate volcanic pumice. Coloured stones and pebbles were also used to simulate marble.

English grotto-owners liked their walls to sparkle, and many made ingenious use of green bottle-glass, mica chips and shards of 'looking-glass'. Crystalline minerals were popular: Thomas Goldney is said to have employed a number of quarrymen for several years to corner the local market in 'Bristol diamonds', a local sparkling crystalline mineral (calcite), which he used to decorate the columns supporting the roof of his grotto.

Artificial stalactites were created by nailing cone-shaped timber formers to the ceiling and plastering them with lime mortar, into which shells and minerals were pressed. At Painshill and Ascot Place the stalactites are covered with overlapping layers of gypsum flakes interspersed with bands of fluorite to give the appearance of water-formed limestone.

Shellwork was for many owners the only acceptable form of internal decoration. The more exotic and unusual the shell, the greater its value. Fan corals, giant conches and pearlised ormer shells were particularly admired and sought after by grotto-owners. Goldney Grotto contains many shells from the West

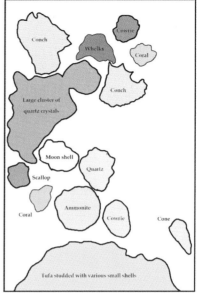

Far left: *Detail of some of the elaborate shellwork within Goldney Grotto, Bristol. This is one of the best preserved of the eighteenth-century shell grottoes in Britain. Over two hundred species of shell adorning the grotto walls and roof have been identified.*

Left: *Identification of some of the shells and minerals in the adjacent photograph.*

Indies, including large corals, geodes, quartz crystals, mussels, fan corals, echinoids and jaspers. Collectors like Mrs Delany and the Duchess of Portland reserved the better specimens for their shell collections and used more common and indigenous shells for decorating grottoes. The Duchess is reported to have gathered thousands of local snails for her grotto at Bulstrode in Buckinghamshire.

Wealthy owners could also commission specialist shellwork from craftsmen like Mr Castle of Marylebone, who had premises at Grotto Lane in London, where samples of his shellwork could be viewed. Castle made his name with a grotto for Sir Robert Walpole at the Royal Hospital garden in Chelsea and is believed to have created the shellwork in the grotto at Wimborne St Giles in Dorset, which Lord Shaftesbury had built in the 1750s as a present for his wife.

A plan of the labyrinth at Hawkstone grotto, Shropshire, showing the intricate rock chambers on Grotto Hill and the dark access tunnel, the longest grotto-tunnel in Europe.

Grottoes were intended to be dark: there are only narrow slits in the walls at Painshill to let in a faint green light from the lake, while at Hawkstone a trained guide had to lead the nervous visitors through the pitch-black tunnels to the top of Grotto Hill, which at 30 yards (27 metres) has the longest grotto-tunnel in Europe. Some grottoes, including Ascot Place, had 'lanterns' or roof lights of coloured glass set into the ceiling, and candle-niches are often found in the walls. The grotto at Claremont Landscape Garden in Surrey has mica-backed niches in the walls for candles, which were lit at

SKETCH PLAN OF THE GROTTO

Above: *At Claremont Landscape Garden, Surrey, William Kent's original three-arched cascade at the head of the lake was modified in the mid eighteenth century to be a grotto, decorated inside with spars and crystals. It was partly restored by the National Trust in 1975.*

Below: *The floor in Goldney Grotto, Bristol, is, unusually for a grotto, constructed from encaustic tiles. The tiles were specially made in Coalbrookdale, Shropshire.*

night to reflect their light on to the waters of the lake.

The floors were usually made of carefully matched pebbles set in mortar and arranged in geometric patterns. At Wanstead Park black and white pebbles were set diagonally, at Stourhead the pebbles swirl in concentric circles, while at Hampton Court House they are arranged in a pentagon to reflect the design of the ceiling. To convey the sensation of being in a real sea cave, the floor at Painshill was covered with fine gravel, sand and oyster shells. The floor at Goldney Grotto is of encaustic tiles in a marbled design of black, red and yellow, specially commissioned in the 1760s from two firms in Coalbrookdale, Shropshire. Polished horses' teeth are used for the floor at Goodwood, and sheep's knuckle-bones at Pontypool in an early, if macabre, example of recycling.

Water was much prized as a feature in or near a grotto. Pope was overjoyed when his excavations at Twickenham uncovered a small spring, which served over the years as a cold bath, fountain and pool. Grottoes often overlooked a lake, and grottoes beside waterfalls were built at Bowood, Wiltshire, and Windsor Great Park, Surrey. At Stourhead, at Stowe, and at Busbridge Lakes, Surrey, the grottoes are constructed over the natural source of a river or spring. Even small grottoes would contain a small internal pool, and the more ambitious owner went in for internal waterfalls, putting great ingenuity into their construction – for example Goldney's steam pump and Hamilton's Archimedes' screw. The grotto at Marlborough has a wall-fountain fed by a head of water piped to the top of the mound in which it is sited.

Many grottoes in the eighteenth century were built as a form of conspicuous consumption – to display the wealth and taste of their owners. Some, like Stourhead, were among a number of classically inspired follies whose iconography was intended to be 'read' by the educated visitor. Owners of a melancholy or reflective turn of mind, like the poets Pope and Scott, used their grottoes for contemplation and writing. Shell houses were often used for light refreshments and some, like Hampton Court House shell house, even had a fireplace. Many grottoes had specially designed furniture. Examples can be seen in the

Left: *Water features were widely regarded as essential in grottoes. This little pool is in the shell house at Endsleigh in Devon.*

Left: *Many grottoes had specially designed furniture. This is one of the original rustic chairs at Pontypool Grotto, south Wales, dating from the early nineteenth century. They were restored in 1997 as part of the general restoration of the grotto by the specialist conservation firm St Blaise Ltd.*

shell room at Woburn and the original rustic chairs from the early nineteenth century are still there at Pontypool.

At Oatlands the three ground-floor rooms comprised a gaming-room complete with fireplace, chandelier and Chinese bamboo chairs, an imitation cave like that at Painshill, and a cold-bath-room with a statue of Venus. Charles Greville wrote of taking a cold bath there during a long summer weekend: 'I bathed in the cold bath in the grotto which is as clear as crystal and as cold as ice.' In 1815 the upstairs room was the venue for a banquet hosted by the Duke of York in honour of the Emperor of Russia and the victors of Waterloo.

Grottoes were also used for housing collections and natural history finds. At the end of the eighteenth century wealthy men and women began to collect shells and minerals, not merely for decoration, but to be studied in their own right. In the 1790s the Duchess of Devonshire commissioned a grotto in the grounds of Chatsworth House, Derbyshire, to house a mineral collection created by White Watson, a Bakewell geologist, for her son, the Marquess of Hartington. The rustic stone hut in the American Garden at Bicton Park Gardens in Devon (1845) still serves as a shell museum today.

One of the most macabre collections must have been the coffin-lids at Wanstead Park, Essex. In the early eighteenth century a masque was held in the grounds at Wanstead. The guests were summoned down to the lake at dusk; as flickering torches illuminated the gathering twilight, the doors of the boat-house grotto slowly opened and a black coffin floated out on to the lake to the delicious horror of the assembled party.

Below: *The late-eighteenth-century grotto at Chatsworth, Derbyshire, commissioned by Georgiana, first wife of the fifth Duke of Devonshire, overlooks the ancient fish stew or pond known as Grotto Pond. The thatched summerhouse was added later.*

Further reading

Arnold, Dana. *The Georgian Country House*. Sutton Publishing, 1998.
Batey, Mavis. *Alexander Pope: the Poet and the Landscape*. Barn Elms Publishing, 1999.
Beckles Willson, Anthony. *Alexander Pope's Grotto in Twickenham*. The Garden History Society, 1998.
Headley, Gwyn, and Meulenkamp, Wim. *Follies, Grottoes and Garden Buildings*. Aurum Press, 1999.
Jones, Barbara. *Follies and Grottoes*. Constable, second edition, 1989.
Miller, Naomi. *Heavenly Caves: Reflections on the Garden Grotto*. Braziller, 1982.
Mowl, Timothy. *Gentlemen and Players: Gardeners of the English Landscape*. Sutton Publishing, 2000.
Saudan, M., and Saudan-Skira, S. *From Folly to Follies*. Evergreen, 1997.
Savage, Robert J.G. 'Natural History of the Goldney Garden Grotto'. *Garden History Society Journal*, volume 17/1, 1989.
Stembridge, P.K. *Goldney: a House and a Family*. Stembridge, revised edition, 1991.
Stembridge, P.K. *Thomas Goldney's Garden*. Avon Gardens Trust, 1996.
Strong, Roy. *The Renaissance Garden in England*. Thames & Hudson, second edition, 1998.
Symes, Michael. *The English Rococo Garden*. Shire Publications, 1991.

Gazetteer of grottoes to visit

All the shell houses and grottoes listed here are open to the public at some time during the year but the opening hours and times may be restricted. Private houses and estates can change hands. You are advised to check opening hours and access arrangements before travelling. An entrance fee is normally payable.

Abbreviations. CHA: Country Houses Association; CT: charitable trust; EH: English Heritage; GGG: entry in the annual *Good Gardens Guide*, available from booksellers; HHA: Historic Houses Association; LA: local authority; NGR: National Grid reference; NGS: open for National Gardens Scheme (check opening times of properties in the NGS 'Yellow Book', available from booksellers and newsagents; many properties which are open all year/season also have NGS days); NT: National Trust; NTS: National Trust for Scotland; PO: privately owned; SH: stately home; VA: visitor attraction (building or garden of historic interest open on commercial basis).

The websites of some of these organisations are as follows: Country Houses Association www.cha.org.uk; Historic Houses Association www.hha.org.uk; National Gardens Scheme www.ngs.org.uk; National Trust www.nationaltrust.org.uk

Telephone numbers have sometimes been withheld by request of the property owner. Four-figure National Grid references are given, as quoted in the Ordnance Survey Gazetteer of Great Britain. They are used with the permission of the Controller of Her Majesty's Stationery Office. In addition to the grottoes listed below, there are many hybrid grottoes: grotto-cascades, grotto-hermitages, grotto-icehouses, and at Mumbles, Swansea, there is a 'grottoloo'. Readers who discover any more grottoes or want to send an update may email the author at HazelleJ@follygarden.com

ENGLAND

Bedfordshire
Swiss Garden, Old Warden Park, Old Warden, Biggleswade SG18 9ER. (LA.) Telephone: 01767 626255. NGR: TL 1444. Website: www.shuttleworth.org Nineteenth-century grotto-fernery.
Woburn Abbey, Woburn MK17 9WA. (SH.) Telephone: 01525 290666. NGR: SP 9534. Website: www.woburnabbey.co.uk Seventeenth-century shell room (Grade I) and nineteenth-century shell house.

Berkshire
Basildon Park, Lower Basildon, Reading RG8 9NR. (NT.) Telephone: 0118 984 3040. NGR: SU 6178. Interior eighteenth-century shell decoration.
Sunningdale Park, Larch Avenue, Ascot SL5 0QE. (NGS. College.) Telephone: 01344 634000. NGR: SU 9567. Pulhamite water garden, rockery and cave.

Buckinghamshire
Stowe Landscape Gardens, Buckingham MK18 5EH. (NT.) Telephone: 01280 822850. NGR: SP 6837. Grade I World Heritage Site. Eighteenth-century grotto and cave.
Waddesdon Manor, Aylesbury HP18 0JH. (NT.) Telephone: 01296 653211. NGR: SP 7316. Website: www.waddesdon.org.uk Nineteenth-century grotto-fountain in aviary; also Pulhamite caves in drive.
West Wycombe Park, West Wycombe HP14 3AJ. (NT.) Telephone: 01494 513569. NGR: SP 7727. Eighteenth-century follies with subterranean chambers.

Cambridgeshire
Peckover House and Garden, North Brink, Wisbech PE13 1JR. (NT.) Telephone: 01945 583463. NGR: TF 4609. Small eighteenth-century grotto.

Cheshire
Adlington Hall, Macclesfield SK10 4LF. (VA and hotel.) Telephone: 01625 820875. NGR: SJ 9080. Website: www.adlingtonhall.com Eighteenth-century shell house. Visits by groups only.
Henbury Hall, Macclesfield SK11 9PJ. (NGS. GGG. PO.) NGR: SJ 8673. Twentieth-century grotto.
Rode Hall, Scholar Green, Congleton ST7 3QP. (NGS. GGG. PO.) Telephone: 01270 873237. NGR: SJ 8157. Nineteenth-century grotto.

Cornwall
Ince Castle, Saltash PL12 4QZ. (NGS. PO.) Telephone: 01752 842249. NGR: SX 4056. Twentieth-century shell house.
Gyllyngdune Gardens, Seafront, Falmouth. (LA.) Telephone: 01872 224355. NGR: SW 8031. Pulhamite rockery and shell seats in seafront glen.
Lost Gardens of Heligan, Pentewan, St Austell PL26 6EN. (VA.) Telephone: 01726 845100. NGR: SW 9946. Website: www.heligan.com Restored grotto-cave in rockery.
Mount Edgcumbe House and Country Park, Cremyll, Torpoint PL10 1HZ. (LA.) Telephone: 01752 822236. NGR: SX 4533. Eighteenth-century shell seat.
Pencarrow, Washaway, Bodmin PL30 3AG. (HHA.) Telephone: 01208 841369. NGR: SX 0371. Website: www.pencarrow.co.uk Nineteenth-century artificial cave in rockery.
Trevarno Estate and Gardens, Helston TR13 0RU. (VA.) Telephone: 01326 574274. NGR: SW 6430. Nineteenth-century grotto-cave in rockery.

Derbyshire
Calke Abbey, Ticknall, Derby DE73 1LE. (NT.) Telephone: 01332 863822. NGR: SK 3722. Eighteenth- and nineteenth-century grotto (remains).
Chatsworth, Bakewell DE45 1PP. (SH.) Telephone: 01246 582204. NGR: SK 2570. Website: www.chatsworth-house.co.uk Seventeenth-century grotto-room; eighteenth-century grotto-summerhouse.
Elvaston Castle Country Park, Elvaston DE72 3EP. (LA.) Telephone: 01332 571342. NGR: SK 4032. Nineteenth-century grotto-cave complex by lake and eighteenth-century grotto (remains).
Melbourne Hall Gardens, Melbourne DE73 1EN. (HHA.) Telephone: 01332 862502. NGR: SK 3824. Website: www.derbycity.com/derby2/mel-hall.html Nineteenth-century grotto.

Devon
A la Ronde, Summer Lane, Exmouth EX8 5BD. (NT.) Telephone: 01395 265514. NGR: SY 0083. Eighteenth-century shell gallery and decoration in house.
Bicton Park Gardens, East Budleigh EX9 7BJ. (CT.) Telephone: 01395 568465. NGR: SY 0785. Nineteenth-century shell museum in Grade I garden.
Endsleigh House and Gardens, Milton Abbot, near Tavistock PL19 0PQ. (PO.) Telephone: 01822 870248. NGR: SX 3978. Grade I nineteenth-century shell house and grotto-tunnel.
Gorwell House, Barnstaple. (NGS. PO.) NGR: SS 5733. Twentieth-century Italianate grotto under construction.
Tapeley Park, Instow, Bideford EX39 4NT. (HHA.) Telephone: 01271 860528. NGR: SS 4729. Eighteenth-century shell house.

Essex
Hatfield Forest, Takeley, Bishop's Stortford CM22 6NE. (NT.) Telephone: 01279 870678. NGR: TL 5320. Eighteenth-century shell house. Visits by written appointment with the Property Manager.

Gloucestershire and Bristol
Barnsley House Garden, Cirencester GL7 5EE. (NGS. GGG. PO.) Telephone: 01285 740561. NGR: SP 0805. Website: www.barnsleyhouse.com Twentieth-century shell grotto.
Goldney Grotto, Lower Clifton Hill, Bristol BS8 1BH. (University hall of residence.) Telephone: 0117 903 4880. NGR: ST 5874. Grade I eighteenth-century subterranean shell grotto with cascade.
Highnam Court, Highnam, Gloucestershire. (NGS. PO.) Telephone: 01452 308251. NGR: SO 7919. Grade 2* Pulhamite water garden with two grottoes in gardens of historic house.
Mill Dene, Blockley, Moreton-in-Marsh GL56 9HU. (PO.) Telephone: 01386 700457. NGR: SP 1634. Twentieth-century shell grotto.
Sezincote, Moreton-in-Marsh GL56 9AW. (HHA.) NGR: SP 1832. Nineteenth-century Mogul-style garden with grottoes.
Stancombe Park, Stinchcombe, Dursley GL11 6AU. (PO.) Telephone: 01453 542815. NGR: ST 7397. Nineteenth-century garden with grottoes and tunnels. Parties only – by appointment.
Warmley Historic Gardens, Kingswood, Bristol. (CT.) Telephone: 0117 967 5711. NGR: ST 6874. Underground eighteenth-century grotto being restored as part of Kingswood Heritage Museum project.

Hampshire
Hordle Walhampton School, Lymington SO41 5ZG. (NGS. Private school.) NGR: SZ 3395. Eighteenth-century shell house. Visits by appointment only.
Staunton Country Park, Middle Park Way, Havant PO9 5HB. (LA.) Telephone: 023 9245 3405. NGR: SU 7310. Website: www.hants.gov.uk Eighteenth-century flint grotto.
West Green House, Hartley Wintney, Hook RG27 8JB. (NGS. NT leased.) Telephone: 01252 844611. NGR: SZ 7456. Twentieth-century grotto by Quinlan Terry.

Herefordshire
Dinmore Manor, Hereford HR4 8EE. (PO.) Telephone: 01432 830322. NGR: SO 4851. Early twentieth-century grotto.
Hampton Court House, Hope-under-Dinmore, Leominster HR6 0PN. (PO.) Telephone: 01568 797777. NGR: SO 5252. Late-twentieth-century tunnel and hermit's cave.
Kingstone Cottages, Weston-under-Penyard, Ross-on-Wye. (PO.) Telephone: 01989 565267. NGR: SO 6324. Late-twentieth-century shell grotto.
Stockton Bury Gardens, Kimbolton, Leominster HR6 0HB. (PO.) Telephone: 01568 613432. NGR: SO 5161. Website: www.countryside-attractions.co.uk Twentieth-century grotto.

Hertfordshire
Ashridge, Ringshall, Berkhamsted HP4 1NS. (NT. Management college.) Telephone: 01442 843491. NGR: SP 9912. Nineteenth-century flint grotto and tunnel.
Scott's Grotto, Scotts Road, Ware SG12 9JQ. (CT.) Telephone: 01920 464131 (hon. curator). NGR: TL 3513. Website: www.scotts-grotto.org Grade I eighteenth-century subterranean shell grotto.

Kent
Belmont Park, Throwley, Faversham ME13 0HH. (CT.) Telephone: 01795 890202. NGR: TQ 9856. Website: www.swale.gov.uk Nineteenth-century rockwork arbour.
Groombridge Place, Tunbridge Wells TN3 9QG. (PO.) Telephone: 01892 863999 or 861444. NGR: TQ 5337. Twentieth-century tufa grotto.
Hever Castle, Edenbridge TN8 7NG. (HHA.) Telephone: 01732 865224. NGR: TQ 4745. Website: www.hevercastle.co.uk Early-twentieth-century Italianate grotto-walk.
Leeds Castle, Maidstone ME17 1PL. (VA.) Telephone: 01622 765400. NGR: TQ 8353. Website: www.leeds-castle.co.uk Late-twentieth-century subterranean shell grotto under maze.
Margate Shell Grotto, Grotto Hill, Margate CT9 2BU. (VA.) Telephone: 01843 220008. NGR: TR 3469. Eighteenth-century or earlier Grade I subterranean shell grotto.
Ship on Shore Grotto, Marine Parade, Sheerness. (Licensed premises.) NGR: TQ 9374. Nineteenth-century rockwork grotto; now part of a public house.

Leicestershire
Belvoir Castle, Grantham NG32 1PD. (SH.) Telephone: 01476 870262. NGR: SK 8233. Website: www.belvoircastle.com Early-nineteenth-century stonework grotto with rustic hut in private gardens. View by written appointment with Estate Office.

London and Middlesex
Battersea Park, Battersea, London SW11. (LA.) NGR: TQ 2777. Pulhamite rockwork.

Chiswick House, Burlington Lane, Chiswick W4 2RP. (LA/EH.) Telephone: 020 8995 0508. NGR: TQ 2177. Early-eighteenth-century 'rustic' pavilion.

Hampton Court House, Hampton. (PO.) Telephone: 020 8892 0221. NGR: TQ 1569. Grade II* eighteenth-century shell house. Visits by appointment with Curator of Orleans House, Twickenham.

Marble Hill Park, Richmond Road, Twickenham TW1 2NL. (EH.) Telephone: 020 8893 5115. NGR: TQ 1773. Eighteenth-century subterranean grotto (partly restored).

Osterley Park, Isleworth TW7 4RB. (NT.) Telephone: 020 8232 5050. NGR: TQ 1478. Website: www.osterleypark.org.uk Grotto area under stairs of rear entrance.

Pope's Grotto, Pope's Villa, 19 Cross Deep, Twickenham TW1 4QG. (Private school.) NGR: TQ 1672. Visit only by written appointment with the headmaster of St James' Independent School for Boys. Telephone: 020 8892 2002. Eighteenth-century Grade I grotto-tunnel.

Wanstead Park, London E11. (LA.) Telephone: 020 8508 0028. NGR: TQ 4187. Eighteenth-century boathouse grotto (ruined).

Norfolk
Queen Alexandra's Nest, Sandringham House, Sandringham PE35 6EN. (NGS. Royal residence.). Telephone: 01553 772675. NGR: TF 6928. Nineteenth-century grotto seat overlooking lake.

Northamptonshire
The Menagerie, Horton, Northampton NN7 2BX. (GGG. PO.) Telephone: 01604 870957. NGR: SP 8253. Late-twentieth-century shell grotto in restored folly.

Northumberland
Cragside, Rothbury, Morpeth NE65 7PX. (NT.) Telephone: 01669 620150. NGR: NU 0702. Nineteenth-century grotto-tunnels.

Nottinghamshire
Carr Bank Park, Mansfield NG18 2AL. (LA.) Telephone: 01623 463245. NGR: SK 5462. Restored nineteenth-century grotto in public park.

Oxfordshire
Hill Court, Tackley, Kidlington OX5 3AQ. (PO.) Telephone: 01869 331221. NGR: SP 4720. Eighteenth-century stone grotto. Enquiries to Court Farm.

Shropshire
Acton Burnell, Shrewsbury. NGR: SJ 5301. Eighteenth-century beehive-shaped shell house on hill.

Brownhill House, Ruyton Eleven Towns, Shrewsbury SY4 1LR. (NGS. PO.) Telephone: 01939 261121. NGR: SJ 3922. Late-twentieth-century grotto.

Hawkstone Historic Park and Follies, Weston-under-Redcastle, Shrewsbury SY4 5UY. (VA.) Telephone: 01939 200611. NGR: SJ 5728. Website: www.hawkstone.co.uk Eighteenth- and nineteenth-century grotto-complex in Grade I park.

Somerset
Banwell Caves, Banwell. (PO.) Telephone: 01934 820516. NGR: ST 3858. Early-nineteenth-century folly garden with caves.

Bath Spa Hotel, Sydney Road, Bath BA2 6JF. (Hotel.) Telephone: 01225 444424. NGR: ST 7564. Early nineteenth-century rockwork grotto.

Crowe Hall, Widcombe Hill, Bath BA2 6AR. (PO.) Telephone: 01225 310322. NGR: ST 7664. Nineteenth-century shell grotto.

Prior Park Landscape Garden, Ralph Allen Drive, Bath BA2 5AH. (NT.) Telephone: 01225 833422. NGR: ST 7663. Eighteenth-century grotto (ruined).

Staffordshire
Biddulph Grange, Biddulph ST8 7SD. (NT.) Telephone: 01782 517999. NGR: SJ 8959. Nineteenth-century grotto-tunnel.

Surrey
Albury Park, Albury, Guildford GU5 9BB. (CHA. NGS.) Telephone: 01483 202964. NGR: TQ 0647. Mid-seventeenth-century tunnel and bath-house grotto.

Busbridge Lakes, Hambledon Road, Godalming GU8 4AY. (PO.) Telephone: 01483 421955. NGR: SU 9742. Website: www.busbridgelakes.co.uk Early-nineteenth-century shell grotto (no access).

Carshalton House, Pound Street, Carshalton SM5 3PS. (Convent.) Telephone: 020 8770 4781. NGR: TQ 2764. Eighteenth-century grotto-hermitage.

Carshalton Park, Carshalton. (LA.) Telephone (Local Heritage Centre): 020 8770 4297. NGR: TQ 2764. Derelict early-eighteenth-century grotto on a hill behind the town centre.

The gardens at Elvaston Castle, Derbyshire, were built for the reclusive fourth Earl of Harrington in the early nineteenth century. When they were opened to the public by his heirs, visitors flocked to see the spectacular topiary and follies. Around the lake a good deal of rustic rockwork has survived, including this large grotto-complex. It was made by using a composition of crushed tufa and gritstone.

Clandon Park, West Clandon, Guildford GU4 7RQ. (NT.) Telephone: 01483 222482. NGR: TQ 0451. Eighteenth-century *nymphaeum*.
Claremont Landscape Garden, Esher KT10 9JG. (NT.) Telephone: 01372 467806. NGR: TQ 1263. Eighteenth-century grotto in Grade I garden.
Painshill Landscape Garden, Cobham KT11 1JE. (CT.) Telephone: 01932 868113. NGR: TQ 0959. Large eighteenth-century artificial limestone cave complex in Grade I garden.

Sussex
Goodwood House, Goodwood, Chichester PO18 0PX. (SH.) Telephone: 01243 755048. NGR: SU 8808. Website: www.goodwood.co.uk Eighteenth-century shell house, Grade I. Visit by written appointment with Estate Office.
Selehurst, Lower Beeding, Horsham RH13 6PR. (NGS. GGG. PO.) Telephone: 01403 891501. NGR: TQ 2126. Gothick folly tower lined with shells. Open one day in May annually for NGS.

Warwickshire
Arbury Hall, Nuneaton CV10 7PT. (HHA.) Telephone: 024 7638 2804. NGR: SP 3389. Eighteenth-century grotto.
Bath House, Walton, Stratford-upon-Avon. (Landmark Trust.) Telephone: 01628 825925 (Landmark Trust). NGR: SP 2853. Website: www.landmarktrust.co.uk Eighteenth-century shell-decorated sitting-room over bath-house. Only those staying at the property are allowed to visit.

Wiltshire
Bowood House and Gardens, Calne SN11 0LZ. (SH.) Telephone: 01249 812102. NGR: ST 9770. Website: www.bowood.org Late-eighteenth-century cave-complex around cascade.
Larmer Tree Gardens, Rushmore Estate, Tollard Royal, Salisbury SP5 5PT. (PO.) Telephone: 01725 516228. NGR: ST 9417. Late-twentieth-century grotto.
Merlin's Mound, Marlborough College, Marlborough SN8 1PA. (Public school.) Telephone: 01672 513989 (tourist office). NGR: SU 1868. Early-eighteenth-century shell grotto in mound.
Old Wardour Castle, Tisbury, Salisbury SP3 6RR. (EH.) Telephone: 01747 870487. NGR: ST 9326. Late-eighteenth-century rock grotto.
Stourhead Landscape Garden, Warminster BA12 6QD. (NT.) Telephone: 01747 841152. NGR: ST 7734. Mid-eighteenth-century *nymphaeum* in Grade I park.

Worcestershire
Croome Landscape Park, Severn Stoke, Worcester WR8 9JS. (NT.) Telephone: 01905 371006. NGR: SO 8744. Website: www.ntrustsevern.org.uk Eighteenth-century grotto (remains). Visit by written appointment with Property Manager, Croome Park, NT Estate Office, The Builders' Yard, High Green, Severn Stoke, Worcester WR8 9JS.
Kyre Park Gardens, Tenbury Wells WR15 8RP. (PO.) Telephone: 01885 410247. NGR: SO 6263. Twentieth-century grotto.

Yorkshire
Bierley Woods, Bierley Lane, Bradford BD4 6QA. NGR: SE 1729. Substantial eighteenth-century grotto-cascade (ruined).
The Forbidden Corner, Tupgill Park Estate, Coverdale, Middleham, Leyburn DL8 4TJ. (VA.) Telephone: 01969 640638. NGR: SE 0683. Website: www.yorkshirenet.co.uk Twentieth-century folly garden and grottoes.
Hackfall Wood, Grewelthorpe. (Woodland Trust.) Telephone: 01439 788206. NGR: SE 2376. Eighteenth-century grotto (ruined).
Oakworth Park, Oakworth. (LA.) NGR: SE 0439. Nineteenth-century concrete and stone grottoes and tunnels.
Skipton Castle, Skipton BD23 1AQ. (VA.) Telephone: 01756 792442. NGR: SD 9952. Website: www.skiptoncastle.co.uk Seventeenth-century shell room.
Studley Royal, Ripon HG4 3DY. (NT.) Telephone: 01765 608888. Website: www.fountainsabbey.org.uk NGR: SE 2770. Eighteenth-century tunnel cave.

WALES
Bedwellty House Gardens, Bedwellty House, Bedwellty Park, Tredegar, Blaenau Gwent NP22 3XN. (LA.) Telephone: 01495 722325. NGR: SO 1408. Nineteenth-century grotto.
Bro Meigan Gardens, Eglwyswrw, Boncath, Pembrokeshire SA37 0JE. (VA.) Telephone: 01239 841232. NGR: SN 1536. Shell grotto.
Brynkinalt, Chirk, Wrexham LL14 5NS. (VA.) Telephone: 01691 778033. NGR: SJ 3037. Website: www.brynkinalt.com Nineteenth-century tunnel.
Glansevern Hall Gardens, Glansevern, near Welshpool, Powys SY21 8AH. (PO.) Telephone: 01686 640200. NGR: SJ 1900. Nineteenth-century rock grotto.
Gnoll Country Park, Neath. (LA.) Telephone: 01639 635808. NGR: SS 7697. Website: www.neath-porttalbot.gov.uk/attractions/gnoll-country-park.html Eighteenth-century cascades and grotto.
Nantclwyd Hall, Pwllglas, Ruthin, Denbighshire. (PO.) Telephone: 01824 703985. NGR: SJ 1258. Twentieth-century grotto. View by written appointment.
Piercefield Picturesque Walk, Chepstow, Monmouthshire. NGR: ST 5394. Follow Wye river walk; start half a mile north of Chepstow on A466. Grotto-cave in eighteenth-century picturesque walk.
Plas Newydd, Hill Street, Llangollen, Denbighshire LL20 8AW. (LA.) Telephone: 01978 861314. NGR: ST 2141. Website: www.llangollen.com/plas.html Nineteenth-century arbour.
Pontypool Grotto, Pontypool Park, Pontypool, Torfaen. (LA.) Telephone: 01495 750236. NGR: SO 2800. Nineteenth-century shell house in grounds of leisure centre.
Portmeirion, Penrhyndeudraeth, Gwynedd LL48 6ET. (VA.) Telephone: 01766 770000. NGR: SH 5937. Website: www.portmeirion.wales.com Twentieth-century shell grotto.
Stackpole Gardens, Stackpole Estate, Bosherston, Pembrokeshire. (NT.) Telephone: 01646 661359. NGR: SR 9995. Eighteenth-century grotto cave.

SCOTLAND
Ascog Hall, Isle of Bute. (PO.) Telephone: 01700 504555. NGR: NS 1062. Nineteenth-century grotto-fernery.
Dunnottar Shell House, Dunnottar Woods, Stonehaven, Aberdeenshire. (NTS.) Telephone: 01569 764444. NGR: NO 8883. Eighteenth-century shell house.
Gosford House, Longniddry, East Lothian EH32 0PX. (SH.) Telephone: 01875 870201. NGR: NT 4578. Eighteenth-century grotto-entrance to icehouse.
Kelburn Country Centre, Fairlie, North Ayrshire KA29 0BE. (VA.) Telephone: 01475 568121. NGR: NS 2158. Website www.kelburncountrycentre.com Twentieth-century grotto.
Newhailes House, Newhailes Estate, Musselburgh, East Lothian EH21 6RY. (NTS.) Telephone: 0131 665 1546. NGR: NT 3272. Late-eighteenth-century shell grotto.
St Ossian's Cave and Hermitage, Dunkeld, Perth and Kinross. (NTS.) Telephone: 0131 226 5922. NGR: NO 0142. Eighteenth-century picturesque walk with hermitage, folly and cave.